I0709881

Trigger Toolbox

A Mental Health Field Guide

By: Willow Grimm

This work is covered by a **Creative Commons Attribution-Non-Commercial** license. This license allows others to remix, adapt, and build upon this work non-commercially.

Publisher Information:
Website: www.libertyunderattack.com
Contact: shane@libertyunderattack.com

Cover Design By: Miriam Zachariah
Interior Design By: Shane Radliff

Published By *Liberty Under Attack Publications*, February 2023

Dedicated to all the survivors out there desperately searching for some solid ground, a torch in the darkness to lead you to someplace that resembles peace.

To my husband who has walked with me in the darkness knowing I had to find my own way out, but refusing to leave my side as I searched and stumbled down dead end paths.

To my mother who gave me a taste of home to remind me what I was searching for when I felt like giving up. From the depths of my heart, thank you for giving me something to fight for.

Managing the symptoms of trauma whether it be a one-time event, a cluster, or childhood trauma, is hard. There's no way around it, you can't run forever, and it always catches up to you eventually. It's also strenuous on relationships, employment, and our own self esteem leading to isolation, depression, and a whole slew of more problems to face each and every day with no end in sight. I know how hard it is because I'm still doing it myself.

This is a culmination of the techniques I use to manage my own depression, anxiety, and CPTSD. Not everything is going to work for everyone else. There are even days when my go-to techniques don't work for me and I have to try out a different one. These are simply my own personal experiences passed along in the hopes that it helps you. I do not take credit for coming up with any of the ideas shared in this book as I found them elsewhere throughout my journey to heal myself. Some were given to me by past therapists, some I read in books and some I've long forgotten where I picked it up. My goal is to pass along everything I've found useful so far to you so that I can shed a little light in this dark forest we call the path to healing.

Table of Contents

Mantras.

Words are powerful. The words you speak to yourself put into motion actions which shape our perceptions of reality. Speaking ill of ourselves can cause illness of the mind and body. Speaking of hope and determination gives us motivation to succeed as seen with the placebo effect. It may not seem like much and often it's hard to see noticeable change until after the fact, but it does make the difference in the grand scheme. My suggestion is to take a few of these, write them down and put them where you can see them every day.

- Every Day
    - One breath at a time, one step at a time, and you will find yourself miles from where you began.
    - Slow is smooth, smooth is fast
    - "Boundaries are the distance from which I can love me and you simultaneously." - Prentis Hemphill
    - I am not alone in my suffering. This is a normal response to an abnormal situation.
    - Even the darkest night will end and the sun will rise.

- I do not blame myself for my childhood experiences/trauma. My mind & body belong to me (or God if you're religious). I release the feeling of guilt, hurt and shame. I deserve to be respected and treated with love. My inner-child awaits to be acknowledged. Today I will comfort my inner child.
- My VOICE is my Power. If I can breathe, I can talk, if I can talk I can sing. My voice is a unique contribution to the world. My body is open and free to express my voice. I trust the brilliance that comes through my voice.
- The more I work on myself, the better my relationships will be. I am not responsible for anyone else's actions, we are all guided by our own consciousness. My world overflows with loving relationships. All the love I seek from without, already exists within. I am able to address any issues within my relationships.
- I choose to be patient with and kind to myself today. My patience is valuable to me and others. I possess patience and understanding. I am patient with allowing forgiveness for myself.

- I'm allowed to take time to heal. I am functioning as I was designed to. I have the power to create change. To make small steps toward big goals is progress.

- ▾ Faith-Based
  - She is clothed in strength and dignity, and she laughs without fear of the future. - Proverbs 31:25
  - Be still and know that I am God. - Psalm 46:10
  - Walk by faith.
  - "For I know the plans I have for you," declares the Lord, "plans to prosper you and not to harm you, plans to give you hope and a future… - Jeremiah 29:11
  - "And Jesus looking upon them saith, 'with men it is impossible but not with God for with God all things are possible.'" – Mark 10;27
  - "Therefore I tell you, do not worry about your life, what you will eat or drink; or about your body, what you will wear. Is not life more than food, and the body more than clothes? Look at the birds of the air: They do not sow or reap or gather into barns-and yet your heavenly Father feeds them. Are you not much more valuable than they?…" - Matthew 6:25

▾ **Gratitude**
The following are Gratitude affirmations.
Repeat seven times.

- I am grateful for the gifts I receive from others.
- My heart holds gratitude toward others and myself.
- I am open to receiving and giving love.

Bring to mind 3-5 things you're grateful for in your life.

- For me, it's being able to pet the stray cat who comes to my porch when it rains.
- Having good friends who I can talk to about most things.
- That storms make me feel happy.
- That I have my husband here with me.

▼ Crisis
- "This too shall pass."
- I tell myself 'that was then, this is now, it did happen, but it will not anymore."

Grounding Techniques.

▼ 1-5 breathing
Breathe in for 1 second
Breathe out for 1 second
Breathe in for 2 seconds
Breathe out for 2 seconds
Breathe in for 3 second
Breathe out for 3 seconds
Breathe in for 4 seconds
Breathe out for 4 seconds
Breathe in for 5 seconds
Breathe out for 5 seconds

▼ 4-6 breathing
Inhale for 4 seconds
Exhale for 6 seconds
Repeat for 3 to 5 minutes or until calmer

▼ 5-4-3-2-1 method
Working backward from 5, use your senses to list things you notice around you.
Five things you can hear,
Four things you can see,
Three things you can touch from where you're sitting,
Two things you can smell,
One thing you can taste.

▾ Take a short walk

Concentrate on your steps - you can even count them. Notice the rhythm of your footsteps and how it feels to put your foot on the ground and then lift it again.

▾ Paint can technique

Visualize an opened can of paint. See the surface of the paint smooth and calm. Overlay the disturbing image onto the surface of the paint. Visualize stirring the paint until the image disappears.

▾ Use math and numbers
Running through a times table in your head.
Do one long division equation.
Counting backward from 100.

▾ Recite something

Think of a passage, poem, or song you know by heart. Recite it quietly or in your head. If you say it out loud, focus on the shape of each word on your lips and in your mouth. If you recite it in your head, visualize each word as if you'd see it on paper.

The one I use the most is *Stopping by Woods on a Snowy Evening* by Robert Frost.

Whose woods these are I think I know.

His house is in the village though;
He will not see me stopping here
To watch his woods fill up with snow.
My little horse must think it queer
To stop without a farmhouse near
Between the woods and frozen lake
The darkest evening of the year.
He gives his harness bells a shake
To ask if there is some mistake.
The only other sound's the sweep
Of easy wind and downy flake.
The woods are lovely, dark and deep,
But I have promises to keep,
And miles to go before I sleep,
And miles to go before sleep.

▾ Pick up or touch items near you

Are the things you touch soft or hard? Heavy or light? Warm or cool? Focus on the texture and color of each item. Challenge yourself to think of specific colors, such as crimson, burgundy, indigo, or turquoise, instead of simply red or blue.

▾ Hold a piece of ice

What does it feel like at first? How long does it take to start melting? How does the sensation change when the ice begins to melt?

▾ Feel your body

You can do this sitting or standing. Focus on how your body feels from head to toe, noticing each part.

Can you feel your hair on your shoulders or forehead? Glasses on your ears or nose? The weight of your shirt on your shoulders? Do your arms feel loose or stiff at your sides? Can you feel your heartbeat? Is it rapid or steady? Does your stomach feel full, or are you hungry? Are your legs crossed, or are your feet resting on the floor? Is your back straight?

Curl your fingers and wiggle your toes. Are you barefoot or in shoes? How does the floor feel against your feet?

Self-Soothing.

- Wash your hands in warm water. Take a warm bath (or shower if you have no bathtub)
- Corner hugs - wrap your arms around your body, press your back into a corner.
- Heart tapping exercise – create a fist, place it directly on the center of your chest, gently but firmly pat your fist on your chest.
- Exhale longer than your inhale.
    (If you have any trauma involving breath restriction or use breath restriction as a coping mechanism, be aware this technique might trigger you and should be used only if it is helping.)
- Massage your shoulders & upper arms.
- Gently hold or stroke your head, arms, upper body.
- Eat (best long-term results if you eat something good for you)
- Cuddle/hug a pet or safe human
- Seek out human interaction with a safe human who understands what state you are currently in.
- Weighted blankets

(If you have a trauma involving being physically restrained, be aware the weighted blankets might trigger that and should not be used to calm the nervous system.)

Assessments.

▾ AM I IN MY BODY?
Can I feel my toes in my shoes or on the ground?
Can I feel my legs and what they are touching?
Can I feel my butt sitting in the chair?
Can I feel my torso expand with my breath?
Can I feel my shoulders and soften them?
Can I feel the places where my clothing touches me or the air on my skin?

▾ **HALT**

When you notice you're having an emotional moment and you find yourself about to react to the emotional state in a way your do not like, ask yourself to HALT, and find out if you are Hungry, Angry, Lonely or Tired. If so, meet these needs before reassessing what you want to do about the emotions.

Everyone has preprogramed instinctual methods of coping with potentially dangerous situations. Most people are aware of the first two fight and flight however many do not know that there are in fact four different stress responses. Often people have two dominant methods but will still resort to the other two if the dominant ones are ineffective. Which ones do you tend to use in moments of high stress?

Fight	Flight
Anger	Anxiety & fear
Aggression	Perfectionist
Agitation	Obsessive/compulsive
Explosive	Overachiever
Controlling	Stays busy
Can't Hear Others	Fidgety
To feel safe: ATTACK	To feel safe: OVERACHIEVE

Freeze	Fawn
Disassociation	People-Pleasing
Shutting Down	Can't Say No
Spacing Out	Little or no self-care
Depression	Lose sense of self in others
Isolating	Co-dependency
	Accepts the bare minimum
To feel safe: ISOLATE	To feel safe: PLEASE

The Four Agreements by Don Miguel Ruiz
1 BE IMPECCABLE WITH YOUR WORD
a. Speak with integrity.
b. Say only what you mean.
c. Avoid using the Word to speak against yourself or to gossip about others.
d. Use the power of your Word in the direction of truth and love.

2 DON'T TAKE ANYTHING PERSONALLY

a. Nothing others do is because of you.

b. What others say and do is a projection of their own reality, their own dream.

c. When you are immune to the opinions and actions of others, you won't be the victim of needless suffering.

3 DON'T MAKE ASSUMPTIONS

a. Find the courage to ask questions and to express what you really want.

b. Communicate with others as clearly as you can to avoid misunderstandings, sadness, and drama.

4 ALWAYS DO YOUR BEST

a. Your best is going to change from moment to moment; it will be different when you are healthy as opposed to sick.

b. Under any circumstance, simply do your best, and you will avoid self-judgment, self-abuse, and regret.

Flags

GREEN FLAGS	YELLOW FLAGS	RED FLAGS
Identifies and respects physical	Lacking awareness or respect for	Demanding physical contact

boundaries	physical boundaries	
Validates emotions while holding accountability for actions	Dismisses or minimizes your feelings	Lack of empathy
Strong ties to a community or social group	Struggles to maintain relationships outside of trauma bonding.	Surrounds themselves with enablers or isolates.
Open to solutions in addition to being heard and validated	Is triggered or invalidated by offered solutions	Victim mentality
Encourages and respects boundaries	Struggles to balance self-care and caretaking of others	People who *take take take* but never give and vice versa.
Allows others to make their own decision even when they disagree without retribution.	Is uncomfortable letting others make decisions they disagree with.	Power plays, retribution for decisions deemed as wrong by one party
Interested in their friends' lives	Struggles to maintain interest in their	Self-centered

	friends lives	
Strong sense of Self	Habit of changing to emulate those they are around	Hyper inflated or no sense of Self
Is not threatened by emotional displays	Uncomfortable with displays of emotions	Shuts down displays of emotion
Requests assistance, time or attention within reason	Consistently dropping things on you without running it by you, or is consistently late without explanation.	Feels entitled to your time and attention. Does not value your time

5 Step Trigger Analysis

NOTICE & NAME

I am feeling________________________________

Sad	Angry	Scared	Disgust	Happy	Peace
depressed	hurt	anxious	disappointed	excited	safe
lonely	rage	insecure	repulsed	creative	open
abandoned	resentful	helpless	awful	free	thoughtful
ashamed	annoyed	shocked	judged	hopeful	content
guilty	jealous	overwhelmed	appalled	energetic	inspired
tired	frustrated	powerless	horrified	playful	trusting
detached	afraid	panicky	embarrassed	curious	satisfied
vulnerable	humiliated	startled	nauseated	grateful	loving

1. PAUSE & WITNESS

Hey ____________. I see you . I feel you. I acknowledge you.

Is what I'm feeling proportionate to the situation?

If no. Then could my reaction be rooted in my past?

2. EXPLORE

What happened? Explore thoughts, beliefs etc.

What am I feeling in my body? Where?
Examples: rapid heart rate, sweaty, headache, nausea, shallow breathing, cold, hot, vibrating, tenseness, palpitations, weird, heaviness, flushed, shaky… etc.

3. PROCESS & INTEGRATION

What core wounds want healed & released?

Identify your Core wounds
I will be abandoned
I am not good enough
I am bad
I am flawed
I am unworthy
I am not safe
I am all alone
I will be betrayed
I will be rejected
I am helpless
I am different
I don't belong anywhere
I feel responsible for everything
I am unseen and unheard
I don't matter
I don't deserve love
I am nothing
I am ugly
I am stupid
I have to be perfect

When should you reach out?

Living with unresolved trauma can often end up leaving individuals drained, isolated, & increasingly susceptible to further re-traumatization. Too often individuals become so used to living with the symptoms of unresolved trauma that differentiating regular experiences and unusual ones can be difficult at best, unattainable at that time at worst, and many shades as personalities in between.

Knowing when or if you should reach out is essential knowledge to have in your tool box. Below is a checklist of the most common reactions to traumatic events and when you should consider reaching out for help.

- ❑ Having work or school problems
- ❑ Feeling nervous, helpless, fearful, & sad
- ❑ Feeling shocked, numb, & unable to feel love or joy
- ❑ Feeling detached or unconcerned about others
- ❑ Having trouble concentrating making decisions
- ❑ Excessive smoking, alcohol, drugs, food.
- ❑ Feeling on guard & constantly alert
- ❑ Having disturbing dreams, images, thoughts, memories, & flashbacks
- ❑ Do you experience trouble with upset stomach or eating
- ❑ Do you experience trouble sleeping or feeling excessively tired
- ❑ Pounding heart, rapid breathing, feeling edgy
- ❑ Sweating without good reason or excessively
- ❑ Severe headaches when revisiting the event
- ❑ Failure to engage in exercise diet, safe sex, regular health care
- ❑ Ongoing medical problems get worse
- ❑ Blaming yourself or having negative views of oneself / world

- ❑ Distrust of others, getting into conflicts, being over controlling
- ❑ Avoiding people place & things for unknown reasons or related to the event
- ❑ Having a disrupted thought process or memory issues
- ❑ Being irritable or having outbursts of anger
- ❑ Being easily upset or agitated
- ❑ Feeling jumpy, Startles easily at sudden or loud noises
- ❑ Being withdrawn, feeling rejected, or abandoned
- ❑ Loss Of intimacy or feeling detached
- ❑ Thoughts or feeling as if your reflection is not quite yours/ not showing the real you.
- ❑ Feelings of hopelessness about the future

If you checked 3+ of the above consistently or struggle with a specific one overwhelming you for a period longer than 6 months, please consider reaching out.

Building a Support System.

1. Accountability

A healthy support system includes someone who can

- Call your bluff when needed,
- Offer honest feedback without you getting angry,
- Help you stay or get back on track.

With no one holding you accountable, recovery can become dangerous. It gives you the room to start justifying behaviors that are not aligned with healing.

2. Fellowship

A healthy support system includes gathering with like individuals who can offer understanding and encouragement and provides a buffer of safety when the process becomes overwhelming.

Be sure to surround yourself with others who are also healing rather than individuals stuck in a victim mentality.

3. Education

A healthy support system includes resources that can offer you information about your issues and on recovery. The more knowledge you have about yourself and what you're dealing with the better you're able to combat it.

If you begin recovery from depression, for example, it is important that you learn why you have depression, how the brain and depression connect, and how to prevent depression relapse. If you know relapse triggers, healthy resources, and positive outlets then you will be well-armed to move forward safely in your recovery.

4. Purpose

A healthy support system includes your sense of purpose. What is the reason you want to continue with this process?

- Maybe it is to help others in a comparable situation.
- Maybe it is to be a better parent.
- Maybe you want to complete a job or project.

Finding your purpose will enable you to stay focused on your healing and give you a reason to continue.

Knowing you have a job to do and a goal to reach helps you focus on something other than your illness and gives you hope.

Purpose directs you to make positive changes in your life, ones that will help you accomplish your goals. It acts as a guide or compass for when life happens and thinking becomes unclear.

Attend counseling so you can have a professional, someone not in your family and not your best friend, guide you through this process. Learn all you can about your symptoms and how to keep them from recurring.

Things to look for in a mental health professional.

A good mental health professional is an individual who is Trauma-informed, practices IFS, EMDR, and has an understanding of shadow work.

The most important aspect of a mental health professional is that you trust them. Meaning you feel comfortable telling them intimate details of your story.

Routine Suggestions.
(Daily for Anxiety & Depression)

- Wake up at the same time every day.
- Go for a walk.
- Eat a big breakfast even if you don't want to, and avoid carbs (eggs, meat, & healthy fats are what I eat to maintain energy).
- Journal.
- Get dressed for the day.

Creating A Day Worth Living
1. Get up early.
2. Express gratitude for what you have.
3. Do something productive.
4. Do something fun.
5. Do something for someone else.
6. Get some sunlight.
7. Exercise - it doesn't matter what, just do some exercise.
8. Put a smile on someone's face.
9. Express gratitude or compliment someone.
10. Learn or do something new.

▾ Once-A-Month (Schedule!)
- 1 lunch date with a friend
- 1 day outdoors
- 1 night out with friends
- 1 breakfast meetup with friends

- 1 movie night
- 1 day serving others
- 1 day completely to yourself.
- 24 hours without social media

▾ Other Suggestions

- Once a week, take a bath with Epsom salts. The magnesium in them absorbs through your skin helping your body physically relax.
- Grow a plant and tend to it each day.
- Give yourself time before bed to wind down and let your body know you're going to bed.
- Walk, stretch, or swim for 30 minutes every day, especially on days you don't feel like it.
- Sit with your thoughts for 10 minutes.

Journal Prompts.

Confronting the Past:
What is a memory I have tried to suppress? How has avoiding it affected my life?

If I could sit with my younger self during a traumatic moment, what would I say or do for them?

The Weight of Shame and Guilt:
What are the things I blame myself for, even if they weren't my fault? Where did this blame originate?

If I could let go of one piece of guilt or shame, how would my life change?

Facing Abandonment and Rejection:
Who are the people who made me feel unworthy or unlovable? How did their actions shape my self-perception?

What would it take for me to believe I am worthy of love and belonging?

The Unspoken Grief:
What losses have I never fully grieved? How does that unprocessed grief manifest in my life?

If I could have closure with someone I've lost—physically or emotionally—what would I say to them?

Reckoning with Anger and Resentment:
Who am I still angry at? What would it feel like to express this anger in a safe, healthy way?

What does my anger protect me from feeling underneath?

Unraveling Fear:
What fears keep me up at night? How do these fears relate to my past trauma?

What would I do differently if fear were not controlling my actions?

Breaking the Cycle of Self-Sabotage:
In what ways do I hurt or neglect myself, even when I know it isn't good for me?

General Health.

I am not giving medical advice, nor suggesting anyone start or stop any treatments without speaking to a medical professional. All of the following information is for you to be aware of and to research on your own as to the effects and uses of each substance. Please speak to your medical provider or naturopathic doctor to decide which are for you and which are not.

▼ 11 Natural Antibiotics
Apple cider vinegar
Capsaicin
Ginger
Onion
Oregano
Garlic
Echinacea
Turmeric
Colloidal Silver
Manuka Honey
Raw honey

▼ 8 Natural Serotonin Boosters
Vitamin B
Exercise
Reduced sugar
Protein
Sunshine

Meditation
Cold showers

▾ Natural Antidepressants
Chamomile
Ginseng
Saffron
Olive oil
Lavender
Magnesium

▾ St. John's Wort
Please be aware that St John's Wort can make many prescription medications less effective, and if a person combines it with antidepressants, a life-threatening amount of serotonin could accumulate in the body.

▾ Curcumin
Curcumin is the main active component in turmeric (Curcuma longa), a golden spice commonly used in Indian cuisine and are as effective for depression as Prozac, the most popular selective serotonin reuptake inhibitor (SSRI).

▼ Avoid
Sugar
Alcohol
Processed carbohydrates (bread, tortillas, etc.)

Nicotine
High amounts of caffeine

▾ **Supplements**
Valerian root
Vitamin B12
Folate
Vitamin D3
Ashwagandha
St John's Wort (can interact with other medications especially antidepressants)

Crisis Contacts.

Write in a contact for each of the prompts to create a list of your support people.

- National mental health hotline 866-903-3787
- National suicide hotline 1-800-273-8255
- A person you can talk to about anything
- A person you can cry around
- A person you can trust to keep the conversation private
- A person you could go see in person if needed
- A person you could ask for a hug
- A person you can trust to hold you accountable & tell the truth.
- A person you can laugh with
- A person who can do a breathing exercise with you.
- A person who will go do an activity with you
- A person who has been through similar trauma or has the same symptoms

Definitions.

- Safe person

A person you feel 100% safe with. Emotionally mental and physically. You will feel yourself physically relax around these people while knowing they will hold you accountable and remain a safe person.

- Mental safe place

An image attached to a word used to recall or experience a visceral state of calm, peace, and comfort. Contact me for a free guided meditation to achieve this.

- Intrusive thoughts

An unwanted thought or image that gets stuck on replay in your mind causing visceral discomfort. These thoughts can be Sexual, Violent, Negative, bizarre, or weird that you do not intend to act upon and do not wish to be present. If you find yourself planning to follow through on self-harm aggressive thoughts, you need professional help to manage your emotions. Talk to a doctor or a therapist.

- Red flags

A sign that indicates a serious problem which must be addressed and resolved for a relationship to remain healthy.

- Yellow flags

A warning sign indicating there could be an issue that needs to be addressed. Can be the result of a mistake, misunderstanding, or trauma or it could be a serious indication of character.

- Green flags

Indication that a person is safe, stable, and potentially trustworthy

- Shadow Self or Shadow Work

Shadow self is the personification of all parts of you that you do not want to be there.
Shadow work is a method of actively trying to see aspects of yourself that you do not wish to be aware of and doing it without negative judgements.

Resources.

- Jordan Peterson books and YouTube, self-authoring course
- *The Crappy Childhood Fairy* on YouTube and Regulation Bootcamp course
- *The Holistic Psychologist* on Facebook
- *Into The Wild Unknown Shadow Work Journal* by Dominica Applegate

About The Author

Willow is a self-taught trauma consultant specializing in sexual and childhood trauma. She works mostly with individuals who suffer from complex post-traumatic stress disorder.

Willow had a difficult childhood, being born December of 1990 to parents who soon after divorced and remarried new partners. After a messy custody battle, she was removed from her mother's home without notice, placed in a group home, and diagnosed with numerous disorders over the following years. As an adult, she has been able to piece back together the fragmented memories of her childhood, sexual abuse, and many other periods of traumatic experiences in the effort to create a life of peace, stability, and wholeness within herself, her marriage, and for her loved ones.

She currently resides in Richmond Virginia with her husband of 11 years, and is dedicated to providing quality care for her clients. She founded *Under the Willow Tree* in 2018, a company determined to bring hope back into the equation when it comes to mental health, healing, and coping with CPTSD.

www.ingramcontent.com/pod-product-compliance
Lightning Source LLC
Chambersburg PA
CBHW051716250726

48653CB00007B/3053